From Sam,

Xmas '0

CW00430731

FRANCIS FRITH'S

LINCOLNSHIRE

LIVING MEMORIES

MALCOLM KNAPP was born in Grantham and, except for National Service, has lived in the town all his life. He was secretary of the Grantham Local History Society for over twenty-three years and is now the President. He is a past Chairman of the Grantham Civic Society and is now a Blue Badge Guide for Lincolnshire – a pleasant change from a career in industry, from which he was made redundant.

FRANCIS FRITH'S
PHOTOGRAPHIC MEMORIES

LINCOLNSHIRE
LIVING MEMORIES

MALCOLM G KNAPP

First published in the United Kingdom in 2004 by
Frith Book Company Ltd

Hardback Edition 2004
ISBN 1-85937-528-6

British Library Cataloguing in Publication Data

Francis Frith's Lincolnshire Living Memories
Malcolm G Knapp

Frith Book Company Ltd
Frith's Barn, Teffont,
Salisbury, Wiltshire SP3 5QP
Tel: +44 (0) 1722 716 376
 Email: info@francisfrith.co.uk
www.francisfrith.co.uk

Printed and bound in Great Britain

Front Cover: LINCOLN, *Stonebow 1923* 74634
Frontispiece: SKEGNESS, *Lumley Road c1955* S134062

*The colour-tinting is for illustrative purposes only, and is not intended to be
historically accurate*

AS WITH ANY HISTORICAL DATABASE THE FRITH ARCHIVE IS CONSTANTLY
BEING CORRECTED AND IMPROVED, AND THE PUBLISHERS WOULD
WELCOME INFORMATION ON OMISSIONS OR INACCURACIES

CONTENTS

FRANCIS FRITH
VICTORIAN PIONEER

FRANCIS FRITH, founder of the world-famous pho-tographical archive, was a complex and multi-tal-ented man. A devout Quaker and a highly successful Victorian businessman, he was philosophical by nature and pioneering in outlook.

By 1855 he had already established a wholesale grocery business in Liverpool, and sold it for the astonishing sum of £200,000, which is the equiva-lent today of over £15,000,000. Now a very rich man, he was able to indulge his passion for travel. As a child he had pored over travel books written by early explorers, and his fancy and imagination had been stirred by family holidays to the sublime mountain regions of Wales and Scotland. 'What lands of spirit-stirring and enriching scenes and places!' he had written. He was to return to these scenes of grandeur in later years to 'recapture the thousands of vivid and tender memories', but with a different purpose. Now in his thirties, and captivated by the new sci-ence of photography, Frith set out on a series of pio-neering journeys up the Nile and to the Near East that occupied him from 1856 until 1860.

INTRIGUE AND EXPLORATION

These far-flung journeys were packed with intrigue and adventure. In his life story, written when he was sixty-three, Frith tells of being held captive by ban-dits, and of fighting 'an awful midnight battle to the very point of surrender with a deadly pack of hungry, wild dogs'. Wearing flowing Arab costume, Frith arrived at Akaba by camel sixty years before Lawrence of Arabia, where he encountered 'desert princes and rival sheikhs, blazing with jewel-hilted swords'.

He was the first photographer to venture beyond the sixth cataract of the Nile. Africa was still the mys-terious 'Dark Continent', and Stanley and Livingstone's historic meeting was a decade into the future. The conditions for picture taking confound belief. He laboured for hours in his wicker dark-room in the sweltering heat of the desert, while the volatile chemicals fizzed dangerously in their trays. Back in London he exhibited his photographs and was 'rap-turously cheered' by members of the Royal Society. His reputation as a photographer was made overnight.

VENTURE OF A LIFE-TIME

Characteristically, Frith quickly spotted the opportu-nity to create a new business as a speciallst publish-er of photographs. He lived in an era of immense and sometimes violent change. For the poor in the early part of Victoria's reign work was exhausting and the hours long, and people had precious little free time to enjoy themselves. Most people had no transport other than a cart or gig at their disposal, and rarely

business one only has to look at the catalogue issued by Frith & Co in 1886: it runs to some 670 pages, listing not only many thousands of views of the British Isles but also many photographs of most European countries, and China, Japan, the USA and Canada - note the sample page shown on page 9 from the hand-written Frith & Co ledgers recording the pictures. By 1890 Frith had created the greatest specialist photographic publishing company in the world, with over 2,000 sales outlets - more than the combined number that Boots and WH Smith have today! The picture on the next page shows the Frith & Co display board at Ingleton in the Yorkshire Dales (left of window). Beautifully constructed with a mahogany frame and gilt inserts, it could display up to a dozen local scenes.

POSTCARD BONANZA

The ever-popular holiday postcard we know today took many years to develop. In 1870 the Post Office issued the first plain cards, with a pre-printed stamp on one face. In 1894 they allowed other publishers' cards to be sent through the mail with an attached adhesive halfpenny stamp. Demand grew rapidly, and in 1895 a new size of postcard was permitted called the court card, but there was little room for illustration. In 1899, a year after Frith's death, a new card measuring 5.5 x 3.5 inches became the standard format, but it was not until 1902 that the divided back came into being, so that the address and message could be on one face and a full-size illustration on the other. Frith & Co were in the vanguard of postcard development: Frith's sons Eustace and Cyril continued their father's monumental task, expanding the number of views offered to the public and recording more and more places in Britain, as the coasts and countryside were opened up to mass travel.

Francis Frith had died in 1898 at his villa in Cannes, his great project still growing. The archive he created continued in business for another seventy years. By 1970 it contained over a third of a million pictures showing 7,000 British towns and villages.

travelled far beyond the boundaries of their own town or village. However, by the 1870s the railways had threaded their way across the country, and Bank Holidays and half-day Saturdays had been made obligatory by Act of Parliament. All of a sudden the working man and his family were able to enjoy days out and see a little more of the world.

With typical business acumen, Francis Frith foresaw that these new tourists would enjoy having souvenirs to commemorate their days out. In 1860 he married Mary Ann Rosling and set out on a new career: his aim was to photograph every city, town and village in Britain. For the next thirty years he travelled the country by train and by pony and trap, producing fine photographs of seaside resorts and beauty spots that were keenly bought by millions of Victorians. These prints were painstakingly pasted into family albums and pored over during the dark nights of winter, rekindling precious memories of summer excursions.

THE RISE OF FRITH & CO

Frith's studio was soon supplying retail shops all over the country. To meet the demand he gathered about him a small team of photographers, and published the work of independent artist-photographers of the calibre of Roger Fenton and Francis Bedford. In order to gain some understanding of the scale of Frith's

FRANCIS FRITH'S LEGACY

Frith's legacy to us today is of immense significance and value, for the magnificent archive of evocative photographs he created provides a unique record of change in the cities, towns and villages throughout Britain over a century and more. Frith and his fellow studio photographers revisited locations many times down the years to update their views, compiling for us an enthralling and colourful pageant of British life and character.

We are fortunate that Frith was dedicated to recording the minutiae of everyday life. For it is this sheer wealth of visual data, the painstaking chronicle of changes in dress, transport, street layouts, buildings, housing, engineering and landscape that captivates us so much today. His remarkable images offer us a powerful link with the past and with the lives of our ancestors.

THE VALUE OF THE ARCHIVE TODAY

Computers have now made it possible for Frith's many thousands of images to be accessed almost instantly. Frith's images are increasingly used as visual resources, by social historians, by researchers into genealogy and ancestry, by architects and town planners, and by teachers involved in local history projects.

In addition, the archive offers every one of us an opportunity to examine the places where we and our families have lived and worked down the years. Highly successful in Frith's own era, the archive is now, a century and more on, entering a new phase of popularity. Historians consider the Francis Frith Collection to be of prime national importance. It is the only archive of its kind remaining in private ownership. Francis Frith's archive is now housed in an historic timber barn in the beautiful village of Teffont in Wiltshire. Its founder would not recognize the archive office as it is today. In place of the many thousands of dusty boxes containing glass plate negatives and an all-pervading odour of photographic chemicals, there are now ranks of computer screens. He would be amazed to watch his images travelling round the world at unimaginable speeds through internet lines.

The archive's future is both bright and exciting. Francis Frith, with his unshakeable belief in making photographs available to the greatest number of people, would undoubtedly approve of what is being done today with his lifetime's work. His photographs depicting our shared past are now bringing pleasure and enlightenment to millions around the world a century and more after his death.

LINCOLNSHIRE
AN INTRODUCTION

HISTORIC Lincolnshire, England's second largest county, is possibly its least known, thanks to the lack of motorways. That has two benefits: firstly, the roads are not choked with transport, and secondly, the locals enjoy a lot more of the peace and quiet of the countryside. That does not mean that we do not like visitors; we most certainly do. We enjoy showing them around our many and varied buildings and lovely and productive countryside, much of which can be seen in this book. Yet we are off the much beaten track. For example, we only have 26 miles of the A1 passing through the county – nearly as much goes through the smallest county, Rutland. Also, after the Beeching cuts only Grantham remained on a main railway line, and the middle of the county is without a railway of any sort. The towns, admittedly small ones (Horncastle, Spilsby, Louth, Woodhall Spa, Alford, Bourne, Holbeach and the twin seaside resorts of Mablethorpe and Sutton on Sea) no longer have a train service. With the increase in the number of cars each year, congestion must be expected soon, especially at holiday times.

Lincolnshire has the oldest canal in England,

the Foss Dyke, built by the Romans. Other towns have or had a canal, but in most cases the canals have disappeared just as some railways have. Gainsborough was a port on the river Trent, and the Brayford Pool in Lincoln was Britain's busiest inland port in Roman times.

After the Romans left Britain, the next group of invaders took over. The Anglo-Saxons were not great builders, but they left their mark in the names of the places where they settled. Later, during the late 10th century, they began to build churches; usually only the tower was of local Lincolnshire limestone, while the rest of the church was of wood. They were built for two purposes: for the glorification of God, and to be a refuge from the Vikings. Lincolnshire possesses more Anglo-Saxon church towers than any other county. The Vikings came intent on rape, pillage and plunder, but eventually they realised how fertile the land was that they were attacking and burning – so they stayed. We now have over three hundred place names that the Vikings brought with them. Some are exactly the same words as they are in Scandinavia; examples are 'toft', and the Mobeck, a small stream which flows through Grantham – exactly the same name appears on a Norwegian map.

Lincolnshire is England's premier agricultural county, and as it is on the eastern side of the country it is one of the driest - hence most of the land is used for arable farming. The usual crops are wheat, barley, potatoes, oil seed rape, linseed and millions of cabbages. Only the land 'set aside' each year is not growing food. There are some sheep, but cattle are not numerous. In the spring, the daffodil is widely grown in the fens, the flat part of the county with spot heights of only one or two feet above sea level. Indeed, Lincolnshire is often dismissed as being wholly flat. The truth is that part of it is, and yet the highest point between London (King's Cross) and Edinburgh on the East Coast Main Line is just south of Grantham and not far from Stamford! The highest place in the county, in the Wolds, is well over 500 feet above sea level.

As the county was engaged with farming and the production of food, the many farmers in Lincolnshire needed the mechanical appliances that were invented in Victorian times. As a result, numerous successful engineering firms were established in several towns in the county. Lincoln had Clayton's, Shuttleworth's, Ruston's, and Robey's; Gainsborough had Marshall's, who occupied the large Britannia Works; and Grantham had Hornsby's, located to the south of the borough in the parish of Spitalgate. All of these factories contributed to the welfare of the local population, and in all cases brought many workers and their families into the towns. The bigger towns of Grimsby and Scunthorpe have both had their industrial problems, with fish wars in Grimsby and cuts in steel production with loss of jobs in Scunthorpe, but it was the development of both places in Victorian times that increased their populations (Grimsby's growth took place earlier than Scunthorpe's). All the firms have gone now, but their legacy is still with us.

The Royal Air Force has always had strong ties with the county, and in fact the RAF College is in the county at Cranwell. In the words of Lord Trenchard, the Father of the RAF, it is located 'far away from the flesh pots of the cities'! The expression 'Bomber County' truly describes

CROWLAND, *The Trinity Bridge c1965* C198048

wartime Lincolnshire – at that time there were more aerodromes in the county than in any other. One very sobering fact is that almost half of the casualties of Bomber Command took off from Lincolnshire airfields, and one wonders how many young men's last sight of England included the magnificent Lincoln Cathedral. The Headquarters of No 5 Group Bomber Command was located in Grantham for part of the war, and Air Marshall Sir Arthur Harris lived in the town for quite a time. In fact, the 'Dambusters' raid was organised from Grantham. In many places throughout the county there are now memorials, which are usually to be found at the entrance to the now lost wartime aerodrome.

However, wars do end, and the survivors resume a normal life. In recent years many have found that Lincolnshire is a less expensive place to live. There are now well over 100 people who commute to London or Peterborough by train from Grantham each day, and many others go to Nottingham.

World events such as wars also affect trade, and Grimsby has had to make a great change since the Icelandic cod war. The town had claimed to be the world's busiest fishing port, which was probably true; but when the cod ceased to be landed at the fish docks, things had to change. By diversifying, Grimsby has now become one of the fastest growing towns in Europe.

Politicians of all hues cause many of the troubles the population have; one that was unnecessary was the nonsensical 1974 boundary changes. Lincolnshire lost its upper part to the make believe county Humberside, cut in half by a mighty river - the Humber. We may be thankful that after many years of complaining the whole of the historic county now does have the name Lincolnshire in its titles - North Lincolnshire around Scunthorpe, and North East Lincolnshire around Grimsby, and a very expensive and attractive bridge over the river.

Lincolnshire is full of history of all periods; indeed, the city of Lincoln put on an exhibition some years ago entitled '21 Centuries of Living History'. I hope you will agree with me that the photographs in this book prove how much of Lincolnshire's living history remains to be discovered and enjoyed.

LINCOLNSHIRE

ADDLETHORPE, *The Church c1955* A319030

St Nicholas' Church and the village are now bypassed from the busy A52 that thunders along towards Mablethorpe. Locally the church is known as 'the Queen of the Marsh'. Its style is classed as early Perpendicular; the chancel was taken down in 1706 and the arch filled in with brickwork. The marsh, the land immediately behind the sand hills, was used by farmers to fatten up their beef cattle on the rich grass that grew there; now thousands of caravans have taken the place of the cattle.

ALFORD
West Street c1950 A209014

The tower of St Wilfrid's Church had to be the perch of the photographer for him to take this shot. The road has not changed, and the route into the Market Place is still the same; however, as in most of these photographs, the telegraph poles have long since gone. The spire of the former Methodist church can be seen in the distance - the building is now a furniture store. The new church is located just behind the older building.

ALFORD, *The Mill c1960* A209027

This is a beautifully proportioned Lincolnshire ogee-capped windmill, which is located on the A1104 road to Mablethorpe. Built in 1813, it is still in working order, and is open to the public regularly. The miller for many years was Mr Fred Banks.

ALFORD
The Church c1955 A209056

Situated by the side of the main road through Alford, the church of St Wilfrid is built mainly of Lincolnshire green stone, which does not wear too well. The road divides a couple of hundred yards further along, with the A1104 going to Mablethorpe and the A1111 to Sutton on Sea. There appear to be no gravestones in the churchyard, but in fact they are there – they are all lying flat. J A Wilson (extreme left), who sold radios and TV sets, has been replaced by Whatnots, who sell curtains and soft furnishings.

ALFORD, *High Street c1955* A209058

The Market Place is to the right. In the distance we can see the shop of Frank and Albert Blakey, grocers, and the High Speed Gas offices. The grocers' shop has now been incorporated into the George public house. West Street, whose sign (right) has now gone, is the route to Horncastle and Lincoln. The road repairs next to the crossing are unusual, as nearly all the roads in these photographs seem to be in excellent condition. The pedestrian crossing has been slightly moved and is now controlled by lights. L W Newman (right) was a butcher, and was replaced by another butcher, Thornalley.

▼ **ANDERBY CREEK,** *Beach Road c1960* A210052

This photograph has a seaside look about it, and it is a breezy and sunny day. The far distant houses are built on the sand hills, and would get the full force of any gales. All that was needed is here: the petrol station is on the left, and on the right Rose's Stores. They would have supplied everything, including Wills Star cigarettes and Coca Cola, according to the advertisements outside.

▶ **ANDERBY CREEK**
Rose's Stores c1960 A210061

Spilsby Rural District Council is stating its presence – see the concrete sign (left foreground). The store is also advertising its wares. There could even have been some Frith postcards in the rack; among many other things for sale are ice cream, Coca Cola, pork pies from Pork Farms of Nottingham, Kodak films, cigarettes, newspapers and Ilford films. William Rose was stated to be a shopkeeper in 1937. The building is still there, but the business is now renting space for caravans, and another Mr Rose (son of William) is the proprietor.

◀ **ANDERBY CREEK**
The Beach c1960
A210067

Here we see one of the famous Lincolnshire beaches with its necessary donkeys. No beach is complete without these loveable and cuddlesome beasts, all with their friendly names. The weather doesn't look too warm, but that will not stop everyone enjoying themselves.

▶ **BARTON-UPON-HUMBER**
St Peter's Church c1955
B750016

The church of St Peter was made redundant in 1972, and is now protected by English Heritage. Lincolnshire possesses very many Anglo-Saxon church towers, and St Peter's is one of England's best. The church could be described as two buildings in one, as part is Anglo-Saxon and the other is 13th-century. This church is a national as well as a Lincolnshire treasure.

BARTON-UPON-HUMBER
Market Place c1955
B750307

Barton-upon-Humber was once a rival to the port of Kingston upon Hull on the other side of the river Humber, but it is now a much smaller settlement, and the Market Place confirms that most definitely. Two buildings at the far end have been demolished for road widening, and even the White Lion (right), which became a pub in 1558, was taken over in about 1970 and is now an extension to The China Shop. The Barton Corn Exchange (the arched building on the left), built in 1853 and opened in 1854, is still there and in use, and in the far corner is an Italian restaurant. The NatWest bank building, built in 1913, is on the left. The Market Place is now mainly a car park and pathway.

◄ **BOSTON**
*Witham Bank and the
Boston Stump c1955*
B155035

The bridge, built in 1848,
carried the Great Northern
Railway main line from
Grimsby to London King's
Cross (via Peterborough),
but since the Beeching
cuts it now only carries
the Skegness to
Nottingham via Grantham
line. The lantern tower of
St Botolph's dominates the
town and the surrounding
countryside. The river
flows down into the Wash.

BINBROOK
General View
c1965 B536027

The church of St Mary and St Gabriel was built in 1869. A far noisier centre was established nearby when RAF Binbrook was built during the Second World War. This was one of the many Bomber Command airfields built in Lincolnshire during those fateful days. A new village, Brookenby, is now located on the old airfield site.

▲ **BOSTON,** *Bargate c1955* B155043

This narrow but busy street is located between the Market Place and Wide Bargate, and is for pedestrians only now - the traffic lights have gone. Some of Boston's largest stores, including Oldrids, are now in Narrow Bargate. Other changes are that Mason's (left) is now Clarks, Radio House (next door but one) is now Dixon's, and Woolworth's have totally replaced the buildings beyond, the Red Lion (there is a commemorative plaque inside the store) and Joan Burns, formerly a dress shop.

◄ **BOSTON**
The River c1955 B155067

This view is looking towards the town centre, and the boat ('BN3', a Boston-registered boat) is heading out to the Wash and the North Sea. The inner relief road, the John Adams Way, has made a tremendous difference to this scene, and only the River Witham is the same. The Boston Ship Stores Ltd (right) has gone, and the building with the chimney in the centre is now apartments. This is the area of the river where the shrimp boats tie up after a day's fishing along the coast.

BOSTON
The Windmill c1965
B155096

Most of the buildings shown here have either gone or been adapted. An exception is the superb five sailed mill, which takes its name from the Maud Foster drain flowing alongside. Buildings to the right of the mill, including R Keightley & Sons (extreme right), are now Mill Lodge, and to the left of the mill is now the Willoughby Grange Care Home.

BOURNE, *North Road c1955* B511009

This is the extremely busy A15 main road heading north to Folkingham, Lincoln and eventually the Humber Bridge and south (the way we are facing) to Market Deeping and Peterborough. The lampposts have changed, and the telephone cables and posts have disappeared. The houses do not appear to have changed, and even the grass verge is still in good condition.

BRANSTON, *The Church c1955* B512002

All Saints' Church was very badly damaged by fire on Christmas Day 1962. The large east window, the entire roof and a large part of the chancel stonework were destroyed. This has all been restored, I am happy to say. This is another of the Lincolnshire churches that has Anglo-Saxon long and short stone work in the tower.

BRANSTON
*Branston Hall Hospital
c1965* B512007

Built during the years 1884 and 1886 for Lord Vere Bertie, Branston Hall later became a sanatorium and then a home for the retired. It is now the 50-bed Branston Hall Hotel. The round turret by the side of the main entrance with its ogee cap looks very much like a windmill tower.

BRANT BROUGHTON, *High Street c1955* B537006

This is locally known as the back road to Lincoln, and it looks a well surfaced village road. It seems as though the photographer was the centre of attention, as both ladies (left) are smiling for the camera. As usual in those days, the village had its shop, and Brant Broughton also had its own petrol station, just the one pump selling Esso petrol. There is some very attractive brickwork on the house facing the camera.

BRANT BROUGHTON
High Street c1955 B537011

What a tranquil scene - one that has probably gone forever. The three young girls could be sauntering home from school with not a care in the world. They would not notice the milk churns on the stand by the side of the road (left), as they were a common sight then. There was also a blacksmith down the road where there could be horses being shod, and there are no TV aerials. The village water was still probably obtained from the roadside tap on the left.

BURGH LE MARSH, *The Church c1955* B513023

The church of St Peter and St Paul, another of the marshland churches, is located by the side of the A158 main road to Skegness - during the summer this is a very busy road indeed. The church was built mainly in the Perpendicular style. Jabez Goode was an interesting man who lived in Burgh le Marsh in Victorian times. He made a collection of all the local words in his area, and thereby saved for posterity words now long since out of use – words going back to our Viking heritage.

▶ **BURGH LE MARSH**
High Street c1960 B513025

Here we see yet another of the beautiful Lincolnshire windmills; this one was built in 1813. Again it is in the Lincolnshire style, with an ogee cap and five sails. The photographer is facing inland towards the village centre where the cattle market and the market place were at the time. They are not there now - housing or car parks have taken their place. The road is still the A158 Lincoln to Skegness road. Remember Green Shield Stamps? The garage on the right offered them!

◄ THE MONCKS ARMS HOTEL
Caenby Corner 1953 G205008

This building is now derelict. A sign of the times is here in the form of the AA box (right) with two AA patrol men going across the road for a quick one! The three men wearing peaked caps (centre right) could well be airmen from one of several nearby airfields; one of them, Hemswell, is now a very large antiques centre. The signpost (left) is a mass of information; there is now a large traffic island at this dangerous cross roads. The A15 is in fact a Roman road – Ermine Street.

CHAPEL ST LEONARDS
The Esplanade c1955
C427002

This is the village centre, and it holds very special memories for the author. It is more than likely that among the people either getting off or getting on the green Lincolnshire double decker 'bus is the author with his mother and sister ! We had family holidays each year at Chapel St Leonards, and in the days before cars were affordable we went by train to Skegness and onwards by 'bus to the caravan. Cannings (left) are first mentioned in 1930, when a Miss Canning had a haberdashery store; Stow's Stores (right) is still in the same place.

▼ **CHAPEL ST LEONARDS**, *The Parade c1955* C427028

Again we see the village centre, with another of the special seaside shops that sold everything needed for a seaside holiday. This time buckets and spades are visible, and so is the sign for Eldorado ice cream. This has all been replaced by a large brick building divided into small shops.

► **CHAPEL ST LEONARDS**
The Vine Hotel c1955
C427089

The Vine Hotel was certainly the largest building in the village; it was built before the Second World War. The writer seems to recall it being more of a very popular pub than a busy hotel. There were two hotels in the village, the Vine in the village centre and the Grange along Sea Bank Road just behind the sand hills.

CHAPEL ST LEONARDS
Merryfield Camping Ground c1955
C427004

The author and his family have had many a happy holiday on this site. My parents eventually had several vans on this field. All had picturesque names, for instance 'Jasmine', 'Magnolia', and 'Elizabeth', named after my sister who was killed in a road crash. Mr R C Smith was the site owner, shop proprietor and general repair man, and he lived in the White House. South Road is to the left, and the sea is only one field away to the right. The White House is now the White House pub and Restaurant.

CHAPEL ST LEONARDS
The Beach c1955
C427024

This view looks north towards Chapel Point and the Coastguard Station. There was also a Second World War gun emplacement on the point. Again there are houses on the sand hills. The breakwater timbers have a worn look about them, but they still served their purpose, and formed little pools for baby crabs to hide in. Children enjoyed catching them until a big one appeared!

CLEETHORPES
The Beach and the Pier
c1955 C112131

The pier was opened in 1873, and was originally much longer. It was shortened to only 335ft after World War Two. Cleethorpes is a very popular seaside resort, despite being on the estuary of the river Humber and not the sea proper. Someone was doing a good trade in deck-chairs, but it was obviously not warm enough for the gentleman in the middle to take his hat off!

► **CLEETHORPES**
Sea Road c1950
C112123

This road is used by coaches as a dropping-off point when bringing visitors to Cleethorpes, and it does not now look as attractive as it does in the photograph. This short road leads to the promenade and pier.

◄ **CLEETHORPES**
Wonderland c1955
C112137

Wonderland was conveniently situated next to the railway station, and when railway excursions to the seaside were at their height, it was ideal for the day tripper. With the coming of the Beeching cuts, trains to Cleethorpes virtually disappeared, and Wonderland correspondingly suffered - as has the station.

▲ **COLSTERWORTH,** *The Village c1960* C428012

This is Main Road, and it is full of local limestone-built houses. Originally it was the Great North Road, and had numerous inns. The building on the left was the Sun Inn, but now for over 23 years it has been the Old Sun Pottery. The building has been greatly restored. There were at least six inns in Colsterworth at the height of the stage coach trade, but now only the White Lion survives. The Great North Road became the A1 in 1923.

◄ **COLSTERWORTH**
The Village c1960 C428013

The square box of the Co-op building (straight ahead) does not sit well with the older stone houses. The garage next to the shop has been replaced by Ramsey Court, and the stone house is now boarded up. The shop fronts on the left are no more, and what looks like a stone barn on the left has been replaced by a stone house. Acacia Cottage is still the first house on the right. This is still Main Road.

▼ **CONINGSBY,** *High Street c1955* C429002

This is the A153 heading towards Sleaford. The White Bull pub (right) is still in existence, but many of the other buildings have gone, and so have the telegraph posts and school sign (left). There is still a school, but it is much further on and on the other side of the river.

► **CONINGSBY**
Silver Street c1955 C429009

This view is looking towards the High Street, and is greatly changed. All the buildings on the left have gone, to be replaced by more modern buildings and a car park for the doctor's surgery. The hairdresser's (right) with its barber's pole has gone, and so has the Gilbey's Wine sign beyond - that shop is now a modern chemist's. The house at the far end of the road on the High Street is now the Birdcage. This is the route to the RAF Battle of Britain Memorial Museum.

◀ **CONINGSBY**
High Street c1965
C429031

As with the other streets in the village, the High Street has also had more than its fair share of change. The Lincoln Co-op (left) has gone along with part of the building. Barclays Bank beyond has gone and been replaced by Goodwins hardware store. Further on was Hall's men's wear shop, but it too is no more. On the right of the road the Castle Inn is still selling beer; the post office (nearer the camera), run for many years by the late Mr Rickard, Senior, a great enthusiast of watermills and windmills, now incorporates a very good bookshop, the whole being under the control of Mr Rickard's son. The modern building on the right is dated 1960, and is now Coningsby Insurance.

▶ **CRANWELL**
The Royal Air Force College c1965 S483053

This impressive building was begun in 1929 and completed in 1933. Lord Trenchard, father of the modern Royal Air Force, chose the site right in the middle of the Lincolnshire countryside so as to be as far away as possible from the temptations of the big cities. It kept the RAF Officer cadets isolated and marooned in the wilderness – or was supposed to. The passing-out parades all take place here just in front of the building. HRH The Prince of Wales learned to fly here.

▲ CROWLAND
West Street c1955 C198018

The trees of this green island were planted in the late 18th century, and most are still here. This is now a one-way road system, and the van is going the wrong way! There are lots of thatched cottages in Crowland owing to the small town's close proximity to the Norfolk reed beds. One cottage on the right, Ship Cottage, is dated 1784, and the cottage next door is dated 1702.

CROWLAND
North Street c1955 C198026

This is a lovely wide open space with ample room for the Friday market. This photograph must have been taken from the Trinity Bridge. On the left, Parnell's shop is now the Ideal Shop, still selling newspapers. The white shop in the distance is still a ladies' hairdresser's, and on the right under the sunblind there is now Lloyds the chemist's. Notice the superb thatching on the house on the left. Further down, near all the cars, is Frydays, a good fish and chip shop and restaurant.

CROWLAND, *The Trinity Bridge c1965* C198048

The 14th-century bridge was a three-road crossing point all those years ago. Now it is a unique part of Lincolnshire's history. There is a mounting block outside G G William's ironmonger's shop (to the left of the bridge), now owned by Martin Day under the logical name Bridge Hardware. The roof has additional dormer windows. The shop under the blind (left) is no longer a shop, but the white house (centre) is still there. We may be glad that the ugly power line post has also gone.

▲ **CROWLAND,** *Broadway c1965* C198028

The stump of the windmill now has no chimney and is incorporated into the house next door, which is named Mill Terrace and dated 1860. Over the years it has lost one chimneystack. All the telegraph posts have also disappeared. The fence is more substantial now, as it is a tall green hedge. The signpost with all its information (centre) has also gone.

CROWLAND, *The Abbey, East Street c1965* C198045

What remains of Crowland Abbey is only a small part of what was there before the Dissolution of the Monasteries. The remains became the small town's parish church. On the right is the way into the car park of Ye Olde Abbey Hostel (that is the name over the entrance), but the official sign has gone. No 27, St Guthlac's Cottage, is stone built and thatched, and No 23 has had new windows inserted. The nearby war memorial remembering the many local men who were killed during the two World Wars needs some attention, as the names are gradually disappearing. The town lost 64 men in the First World War and 17 in the Second.

DENTON
Church Street c1960
D260006

The village hall is on the left, and so is the school sign for the village school that stands very near to the church. The village has many attractive ironstone cottages – note the ones on the right. The very popular village pub and restaurant, the Welby Arms, is just beyond the road junction.

DENTON, *The Village c1960* D260009

Here we see several more of the local ironstone cottages with their well kept and productive gardens. There is a fine crop of runner beans in one garden as well as the usual flowers. This is a lovely tranquil scene with not a car in sight - it is usually the same today. The road to the left leads to the pub, the school, the village hall and the church, and the road to the right to Sedgebrook and the A52 to Nottingham.

DONINGTON, *The Church c1965* D220045

The church of St Mary and the Holy Rood has many historical connections with Donington's famous son, the great explorer Matthew Flinders. The Australian connection is remembered by the memorial tablet and window given by Australia, and there are numerous gravestones in the churchyard of Flinders's relations. The village bypass is just to the other side of the church.

DONINGTON
Market Place c1965
D220034

There used to be a Saturday market here, but eventually the larger markets of Boston and Spalding took its trade. The A52 leads to Boston, and the A152 goes on to Spalding. Get A Head (a ladies' hairdresser) has taken over from Margaret Graves (left), and the chemist (centre left) is still there. Wilkinson's (centre right) is now Marshall's fruit and vegetable shop, and a Chinese takeaway has appeared. The Red Cow hotel/pub (the white building on the right) has been boarded up for ages, and it needs assistance desperately. At long last the Black Bull Inn (just visible on the extreme) right was being restored and refurbished when this research was being undertaken in 2003.

▶ **GAINSBOROUGH,** *Bridge Street c1955* G145016

Once Gainsborough was a busy port on the river Trent, and Bridge Street runs parallel to the river. Now all of that has changed, and so has Bridge Street, for it has virtually all been knocked down for redevelopment. On the left is now either cleared or a car park, and the road is much wider. Here the river Trent is the boundary between Lincolnshire and Nottinghamshire.

▼ **GLENTHAM,** *Main Street 1953* G205010

Here there is a profusion of telegraph wires and power cables, but no TV aerials. Actually, several more things have disappeared, including the signpost, which has been replaced by much smaller signs that are partially covered by the hedge. No one seems to know when the chapel on the right was demolished; before it was demolished it was used by Mr Taylor for animal food storage. The Crown Inn and Restaurant (the white building to the left of the road) is still there, as are the other houses. This photograph looks towards Market Rasen.

GLENTHAM, *Main Street 1953* G205003

The Crown Inn (right) still looks the same, but the stone wall has been reduced in height. The Hole's Ales advertising sign on the wall has gone, and the beer being advertised on the hanging sign is now Carling. The main change is that the single petrol pump and brick hut have disappeared, and so has the shop front of what was the general stores. The house is now known as Glendower House and is a guesthouse.

◄ **GRANTHAM**
St Peter's Hill c1955 G43042

The large trees have gone, but they were replaced in 2004. The 'bus station next to the library and museum has moved – and so has the library. The privet fence around the green has gone, and the grass has been replaced. The taxi rank could be on the move in the future. Sad to say, nothing looks at neat and tidy as it did in 1955, but it looks a lot better than it did a couple of years ago.

GRANTHAM
*The Angel and Royal Hotel
c1955* G43032

The hotel façade has not changed, but Boots have moved further along the High Street and the Halifax Bank has replaced Boots. Fortunately for the hotel, it has been taken over by a group of local businessmen, and it looks much, much better now. It was needing a lot of attention, and it at last received it, with a lot of money being spent on its restoration. The signs have disappeared, and it no longer has any connection with Trust Houses Forte. It has resumed its place as a most important part of Grantham's and England's history.

GRIMSBY
The Fish Dock c1955
G60019

Grimsby was once the world's largest fishing port, but the 'cod wars' ended that. This is truly a magnificently busy and marvellously nostalgic photograph, showing all types of fishing vessels and cranes, and the Victorian Dock Tower standing a majestic 309 feet over the busy port. The tower was built in 1852, and can be seen for many a mile. The first fish dock opened in 1856, and the Royal Dock was built between 1849 and 1852.

GRIMSBY, *The Bull Ring c1965*
G60057

Oh dear, oh dear! Very little of this pleasant scene is still in being. The bus driver told me after he had seen the photograph that 'it's all under Wilkinson's'. And he was correct. What is left is partially pedestrianised, and a few of the buildings are still there, but not many. The 18th-century Tivoli Tavern (the white building, centre left), formerly the Globe, is still there, but the buildings on the left are no more, having being replaced by Devonshire House. Because so much change has taken place, the Bull Ring was not recognisable; when I asked where it was, the answer came 'You're standing in it !'

GRIMSBY, *Old Market Place 1964* G60076

The car park has gone, and many of the buildings have also disappeared. The Tivoli Tavern can be seen to the left, but Albert Gait has been replaced by the Alliance and Leicester (the gabled building, centre left), and Citi Financial is installed in Pinbox House (centre). The Pestle and Mortar pub next door is closed, and all the buildings on the left have been demolished. It is another case of 'Oh dear, oh dear!' However, the largest shopping mall in Lincolnshire is nearby, and so is the very useful-looking large indoor market.

HECKINGTON, *The Mill c1955* H63015

This is the only eight-sailed mill England, and has just (2004) had its ogee cap and sails repaired and reinstated. When working it is probably the most beautiful windmill in England. Built in 1830, but with only five sails, it was damaged by a storm in 1890. When it was repaired in 1892, the number of sails was increased to eight. The mill is a truly beautiful sight, and can be seen for many a mile across the flat and fertile fen countryside.

◄ **HEMSWELL**
Dawnhill Lane c1955
H316003

The houses on the right were built by the council not long before the photograph was taken, and from their appearance several are now privately owned. The large tree behind the barn has gone, but the grass verge is still in being and in fairly good condition. Opposite the houses is a very busy horse-training yard - well over twenty horses go for walks down the local country lanes.

HECKINGTON
The Church c1960
H63019

The large village of Heckington has two great buildings, the mill and the church of St Andrew, which is most unusual in that it was totally built in the same architectural style, Decorated, in a very few years. Hope Cottage near the church is dated 1888, and at No 16 Church Street a tall tree has replaced what looks like a broken-off post (right).

▲ **HOGSTHORPE,** *High Street c1960* H317004

The Midland Bank is no more, but the flat-roofed building that sticks out like a sore thumb is still there. It now serves as a garage for an ice cream van, and it still has the iron bars over the windows. The first house on the left is named The Old Post Office, and the Old Cobblers Shop is further up the street. The little building squeezed between the two houses (left) is the shop/store of an electrical contractor. The road is the A52.

◄ **HOLBEACH**
High Street c1955 H318047

The Chequers Hotel (left) is still in business, but the Freeman, Hardy & Willis shoe shop next door has gone - the building is now used by Eastern Delight. Hanson's Bakery is beyond in the shop that was Bayston's, who were farmers, purveyors of meat, bakers and confectioners. The Bell Hotel next door is also still there, but the building beyond has gone, being replaced by Lloyds Bank. The entrance canopy of the Chequers Hotel has been removed. Canopies like this get knocked off by lorries, as has been the case at Grantham and Navenby.

HOLBEACH
High Street c1955
H318085

The shop extension filled with shoes and boots is now filled with all manner of things for pets. On the other side of the road was a garage, which is now the Job Centre and the Sue Ryder shop. Then comes the HSBC bank followed by a building dated 1789 which now houses Calthop, solicitors. The pub, the Horse and Groom, is followed by the Central Fish Bar. Finally, nearest the camera stands the imposing building The Chase, which was built in 1846 as a boarding house for boys and the master of the local Grammar School.

▶ **HORNCASTLE**
Market Place c1965
H319040

The Stanhope Memorial stands in the middle of the space where the market is held twice a week. All the buildings have changed proprietors except the big white building with the three dormer windows, which is still the post office. The Butter Market of 1853 (centre) is now Achurch Hardware Store, and the snack bar next door is now a pizza and kebab house. There is a blue plaque on the 1775 town house of Sir Joseph Banks (right). Sir Joseph came from the nearby village of Revesby, and the plants he brought back from his journey with Captain Cook formed Kew Gardens.

◀ **HORNCASTLE**
Market Place c1965
H319045

The two small buildings on the right have been replaced. One was taken down, and apparently the other fell down! Now there is a spate of banks. Boots have changed their location to be in one of the new shops. The white shop facing the Market Place, now the Achurch Hardware Store, was the Conservative Club; B E Lilly to its right has been replaced by Poynton's, but is still a shoe shop. This was Sir Joseph Banks's house.

▲ **HORNCASTLE,** *The Bull Ring c1965* H319041

The thatched 17th-century King's Head pub still stands on the left, and the re-fronted Red Lion Hotel is still in the centre of the Bull Ring. Clark's of Retford next door have been replaced by Mellor's, a local butcher. R L Kisby and the Trustee Savings Bank (right) have gone, and Mills the newsagents have taken their place. The newsagent who was next door has in turn been replaced by Le Strange Emporium, who claim to have 'the largest permanent art exhibition in Lincolnshire'. C Crew (centre right), a gift and toyshop, has now become Horncastle Furnishers.

◄ **INGOLDMELLS**
Butlin's Holiday Camp c1955
I47025

The long-time motto all along the front of the large road-side buildings was 'Our True Intent Is All For Your Delight', which is a quotation from 'A Midsummer Night's Dream'. However, the motto and the buildings have disappeared in an almost total rebuild of the camp. In 1936 it was the first holiday camp to be built in Britain. Locals were most surprised when it was claimed by Lord Haw Haw to have been sunk during the war, when it was known as HMS Royal Arthur and was a Royal Navy training camp.

▼ **INGOLDMELLS,** *Moores Holiday Estate Camp c1955* I47063

This is now Coral Beach, with made-up roads and caravans that look more like mobile homes. This photograph was taken along Roman Bank - which is not Roman at all – and the scene is totally different today.

▶ **INGOLDMELLS**
Moores Holiday Estate Camp
c1955 I47072

Ingoldmells has had millions of pounds spent on its redevelopment, and more is promised for the future. This makes it difficult to recognise a place like this. All that is the same are the steps leading down to the building, which is now two-storey and called Sealands. The adjoining house is now fully incorporated with it and unrecognisable. Nearby is the fantastic Fantasy Island development, with the largest Sunday market in Europe and several white knuckle rides; one is said to be the biggest or highest in England at over 300ft high.

◄ INGOLDMELLS
The Beacon Restaurant c1965
I47090

We are in the village centre on Queensway. The restaurant was closed for the winter here, but it certainly looked neat and tidy and waiting for the rush of summer visitors.

► INGOLDMELLS
The Beach c1965
I47102

How many donkeys are there, and who is in charge? This is holiday perfection, with breakwaters, windbreaks, donkeys, buckets, spades and plenty of sand, plus the bonus of the sunshine. What more could one ask for?

INGOLDMELLS
High Street c1965 I47108

The road is still the A52, with a few bends in the village centre. Skegness is to the right. This part of the village has not changed: the Ship pub is still there on the right, and the line of little shops still stands on the left, but all with different owners. The road straight ahead leads to Fantasy Island.

LINCOLN
Broadgate c1950 L49009

The Drill Hall (left), which was then the HQ of the 4th Battalion Royal Lincolnshire Regiment, has recently had a complete restoration; it reopened on 20 March 2004 to resume its place in the entertainment life of Lincoln. The Duke of Wellington pub next door was built in 1933. Messrs Parke & White of 45 Broadgate (extreme left) closed in 1958, and the site is now the new and expanded Lincoln City Library. The road is now divided, with crossing places for pedestrians. This is now an extremely busy road, and there is a host of traffic lights where five roads meet at the bottom of Lindum Hill, just about where the car is coming down the road.

► **LINCOLN**
The Stonebow c1950 L49021

The Stonebow, which dates from the late 15th century, is where the city council hold their meetings. It is on the site of the southern gateway of the Roman colonia. This area is now pedestrianised, and has greatly changed. The Regal Cinema (left) and the drapers C J Fox & Co nest door are no longer there, having been replaced in 1966 by a Littlewood's store. Kendall's (left) were umbrella makers as well as sellers. Woolworth & Co (right) also moved from the High Street into the Waterside Shopping Mall until March 2004, when they closed down. The late Georgian Saracens Head Hotel beyond stood there until 1959 - it had many wartime RAF connections. Ottakars bookshop is there now. Notice a very scruffy soldier – beret off and hands in pockets (right foreground). My RSM would have had something to say!

LINCOLN
High Street c1955 L49040

This is all pedestrianised now, and no double decker bus is to be seen in this part of the High Street. The High Street is in fact the Roman Ermine Street, and it goes all the way through the city. The sign for the medieval High Bridge Restaurant can just be seen next to the bus. Just as important today as it was in 1955 is the motto 'that one is never too young to begin saving' – note the poster on the left. The bridge, which has Norman work in it, is over the river Witham, and its railings can be seen on the right of the street. It is an unusual and different sensation to be sitting and eating in the upstairs of the restaurant and see a boat go underneath. The block of buildings incorporating the Hotel Central and Lennards shoe shop (right) all have different occupants.

▲ **LINCOLN,** *High Bridge c1955* L49094

The River Witham is narrow here, but deep, as it was probably canalised during Norman or even possibly Roman times - the bridge does include Norman stonework. The medieval house on the bridge was greatly restored during 1900-01. The swan looks lonely; usually there are dozens on the river and the Brayford Pool, which is under the bridge. Marks & Spencer, who came in 1931, occupy the building to the left of the High Bridge Restaurant; Burton's (left) are still there, and have been joined by Dorothy Perkins. The wooden contraption on the right which looks like stairs has long since gone. It was probably useful, but left a lot to be desired architecturally.

◄ **LINCOLN**
*The Green Dragon Hotel
c1955* L49130

This is part of the riverside group of medieval buildings which also includes the Witch and the Wardrobe, which is next door. The Green Dragon was heavily restored in 1958, but was built during the 16th century. The river is still open to holiday pleasure launches going to either Boston or westward to the River Trent at Torksey.

LINCOLN
The Cathedral c1965 L49232

The cathedral is accepted as being one of the most beautiful buildings in Europe; it dominates the uphill area of the city and its surrounding buildings. In front is the Exchequer Gate, which was actually part of the cathedral defences. To its left is the church of St Mary Magdalene, built between 1280 and 1299. Then comes a half-timbered building that is now used as the Tourist Information Office, and then the Judges' Lodging, built in the early 19th century. Castle Square is used each year

for part of the Lincoln Christmas Market, and is often used as a film location. The famous street Steep Hill, the most aptly named street in England, is down to the right. The building facing the square on the right is now a restaurant named The Magna Carta, the best remaining copy of which is on view in the castle.

LOUTH, *Eastgate c1955* L305050

This street scene has not changed very much except for the names of the occupants. The Whyte Swanne of 1612 is still there, and Peacocks have replaced the long-time Louth outfitters of Lawson & Stockdale at No 47(centre). Peacocks also expanded into the Prudential next door. Wilkinson's took over from Fine Fare (right) at the same time as the decorated art work on the pediment above the blank front was lost. Then comes Superdrug on the corner of Vickers Lane (formerly Post Office Lane), and then Argos. Barclay's Bank is still at 64 Eastgate (extreme right). As the railways since Lord Beeching's cuts do not visit Louth, the sign (left) pointing to the station has also gone.

LOUTH
Market Place and Market Hall c1955 L305060

The NatWest (left) has not changed. The Central Café (facing us, left) has gone, to be replaced by New Look. The accountants Forrester Boyd & Co at 7 Corn Market next door have been replaced by Hanson's the bakers, and next door is now the Louth Vision Centre. After the entrance to the Market Hall (1866-67) comes Lunn Poly. Long established locally, Pocklingtons the bakers began in nearby Withern in 1924, and have been here since 1996.

LOUTH, *Eastgate c1960* L305067

The Greenwich Meridian sign on the wall between Nos 105 and 107 is well worth finding - it was placed there in 1948. Both clocks have been taken away from this busy shopping street, but Milletts Army and Navy Store (right) is still there. Even the Hewitt's sign on the side of the Jolly Sailor beyond has gone; the shop is now Vogue, and in 2004 is painted a very bright colour. The corner shop on the left is Superdrug, and the Pack Horse Hotel is still there. The pedestrian crossing has been moved to be more convenient for shoppers, but not for car drivers!

LUDFORD MAGNA
The Village c1955 L509002

This is the A631, although it does not look like an A-class road. The telephone box has gone, and so have the telegraph poles and wires. The post office has moved, and is no longer in the far distance on the right of the road. The annexe sideways to the road has gone, and the house standing back from the road has been replaced by a bungalow. One of the two houses on the right, Highfield View, now has a porch. The wartime airfield was over to the left.

LUDFORD MAGNA, *The Village c1955* L509016

The school with its warning sign is over to the left. The pub in the distance is still the White Hart, but the petrol station has gone. The village church is hidden behind the trees on the right. During the war the aerodrome was under the command of Bomber Command, and 101 Squadron was stationed there for several years. During that time it suffered the highest losses of any squadron, and there is a monument to that effect beside the road in the middle of the village. There are also two seats donated by the squadron survivors.

▲ MABLETHORPE
South Promenade c1955 M1015

Let's go home before the storm! The Lincolnshire coast is well known for its sandy beaches, and Mablethorpe and Sutton on Sea are outstanding, as this photograph shows. There were numerous chalets which could be hired for the day or week along the promenade, and the big wheel is also to be seen in the far distance – it has now gone.

▼ **MABLETHORPE,** *The Beach c1955* M1050

This photograph was probably taken from the top of the big wheel, something no longer possible. Most of this area had been redeveloped after the 1953 storm, and it has since been redeveloped again. Only the concrete steps are still there - all the other buildings and the fun fair have been changed or altered. Even Wally's Roll-A-Ball (left) has gone!

MABLETHORPE, *High Street c1955* M1055

The arrival of the railway in 1877 put Mablethorpe on the seaside holiday map, and the town is mainly Victorian or later. The Book in Hand (left) is mentioned in the mid 1800s, but it was badly damaged by fire in 1981 and the two bays have gone. It was classed as a hotel and lodging house in 1856, and is now an indoor market. The Royal Café (extreme left) is now the Café Royale. The Café Regent in the far distance is no more - the whole building has gone in a seafront redevelopment. Note the many people walking towards the front: it looks as though they have just got off the train (there is no longer a station here) or are walking from the bus station (no longer there), which was to the left of the Royal Café. The brick façade on the right has also been demolished, and the snack bar is now the Mablethorpe Rock Co.

◀ **MABLETHORPE**
Donkey Rides c1955
M1073

This ride seems to have been a fairly serious event. Admittedly it does not look very warm, as there are no shadows and not many people. Nevertheless a donkey ride was a must, and donkeys always knew when it was time to go home, or when to return to the start line once more.

▶ **MARKET DEEPING**
Stamford Road c1955
M116009

This is the A16 coming in from Stamford towards the town centre. Mill Cottage is on the right, and the River Welland is at the other side of the house. The timbers of the upper storey have since been covered over by sandstone-coloured paint. The tiny houses further along the street have been rebuilt into one house with two dormer windows in the roof.

MARKET DEEPING
Market Place c1955
M116018

This is the A15 road coming in from Bourne, which makes the traffic island a very busy place - it is now much smaller than it is in the picture. The attractive Georgian door (left) has been filled in, and Mulligan the tobacconist next door is now Tonino's Pizzeria with a new frontage. The large building beyond is now a Londis store.

MARKET DEEPING, *Market Place c1955* M116040

This area has changed quite a lot, and has adapted to the extra traffic that has occurred during the past fifty years. The space in front of the shops is now a car park, and the traffic island has shrunk. The 17th-century Bull pub (centre left) is still there, as is the Town Hall, but two banks now stand along that side of the street.

MARKET DEEPING
Church Street c1955
M116043

This view looks north along the A15 towards the church of St Guthlac and Bourne. Again, the buildings are the same today - in fact the only difference is the addition of a telephone box in front of Willoughby House on the left. The antiques shop (right) next door to the White Horse pub is no longer in business.

MARKET DEEPING, *High Street c1955* M116061

Market Deeping has been fortunate in that it has kept most of its attractive stone buildings, and this street is still much the same today. However, the use of the buildings has changed, and the Georgians Restaurant (right) became The Laurels Rest Home in 1985. The building is dated 1878. Next door is the Caudle House restaurant.

MARKET RASEN
Queen Street c1955
M231043

This is the main street through the town. The steps used to lead into the post office, but it is now a restaurant and Tourist Information Office. The Corn Exchange next door is still there, and on the other side of the road stands the Gordon Arms Hotel. When the author was researching this book (2004), the road (the A631) was almost non-existent as large road works were taking place, which were due for completion by the spring.

MARKET RASEN
Queen Street c1955 M231044

This view looks eastwards towards the railway bridge that carries the line from Grimsby to Lincoln. Again, the buildings have hardly changed, but the occupants have. Rasen Bikes are in the large shop on the left, which was E C Hall's shoe shop. The White Swan beyond is still there, and next is another shoe shop, E C Hall. A young lady is in charge. Wold Antiques is next, and then comes a building that is looking sad and forlorn. It still has the name Albion Furnishing Stores painted on the side, but it fact it looks very empty. On the right is Union Street; the corner shop was W H Smith, but is now Oxfam. All of this part of the street was dug up during the extensive road works of early 2004.

METHERINGHAM, *The Church c1955* M232001

The church of St Wilfred is another of the hundreds of Lincolnshire limestone churches, and it has not changed in almost fifty years. The church was damaged by fire in 1599 and restored in 1601. Notice the small lancet window – it is the only one. The trees are still there, but are now much taller.

METHERINGHAM, *The Memorial c1955* M232003

This is a well-kept Garden of Remembrance in the centre of this large village; next door is the County Library. There were five wreaths around the plinth on the day I visited, including one from the Parish Council. The statue is clean, and the soldier's cap has a Lincolnshire Regiment cap badge carved on it. On the plinth are the names of 42 men from the village who died during the First World War and 8 from the Second.

81

▶ **MIDDLE RASEN**
The Church c1955
M247014

The church of St Peter, in North Street, has a superb Norman doorway, possibly the best in the county (so the experts say), and the church has further Norman architecture inside. The thatched cottages are no more; the nearest has been replaced by a no doubt very functional large brick house.

◄ **NAVENBY**
High Street c1965 N132009

Navenby now seems to be an almost self-contained village on the A607 between Lincoln and Grantham. The main street consists mostly of stone cottages converted over the years into shops. The Lion and Royal pub (left) is still there (Royal because of a royal visitor years ago), and the Co-op opposite is in a new stone-fronted building of 1996. The bus shelter has moved, but the red telephone box is still in use. In 2004 the Home Grown Cereals Authority awarded the Navenby bakers Pete and Mary Welbourn the first prize in the Tasty Baker Award scheme. Their shop (next to the Co-op) is now wheelchair-friendly, a very useful asset.

◀**NORTH SOMERCOTES**
The Lakeside Lido Club Bar c1955 N131039

Things change during fifty years. This photograph proved it beyond any doubt as all this has gone, even the building which contained it. The demolition took place about five or six years ago, no one was quite sure when, but the one thing that was said positively was that the replacement is better!

NAVENBY
The Church c1965
N132010

This is another of the Lincolnshire churches built with the local limestone. It overlooks the Trent and Witham valley towards the Nottinghamshire border. The tower of the church of St Peter was rebuilt in the 18th century after the previous one fell down. The church has been modernised recently with the addition of a kitchen and toilets, very useful additions. The path between the hedge and the stone wall is named the Cat Walk.

▲ **REVESBY,** *The Green c1955* R306007

Revesby is an estate village, and the Estate Office on is the nearby A153 main road. The village was laid out in the 1850s around a huge green. It was all done in memory of Sir Joseph Banks, who lived in Revesby Abbey, named after the 12th-century abbey, a Cistercian foundation. The school (right), now converted into two houses, was built in 1858. The house with the shop front facing the camera is now named the Old Post Office.

◄ SALTFLEET
Sea Lane c1955 S479021

The lane just stops here, but not at the sea –beyond is an RAF bombing range. There are danger signs and red flags all over the place. Caravans are now in all the spare spaces, and the wooden huts (right) have been replaced by a modern brick building. The house on the left is in the process of being altered (2004), and the lean-to has already gone.

▶ **SALTFLEET**
Main Road and the Village Centre c1965 S479059

There are now no shops on this corner. Traffords Stores (right) is now a house, and so is the General Stores (left), where both the window and door are bricked up. The Crown Inn is on the extreme right behind the trees.

◀ **SALTFLEET**
The New Inn c1965 S479062

The reason for the name is that the front part of the inn is the new part - it was added onto the existing part in the 18th century. There is now a brick extension that has been added behind the 'new' part going up the driveway that leads to the office of a caravan letting firm. The fruit tree climbing up the wall is still there, and so is what looks like a mounting block.

▲ **SALTFLEET,** *Main Road c1965* S479064

The windmill was built in the 1770s and largely rebuilt in the 1890s. It has been converted into a living area and added to a house; it has had an ogee cap fitted to it, but no sails yet. The Windmill Garage and Store (centre left) now supplies UK Petroleum. This is the A1031 coastal road to Grimsby, with the sea to the right.

◄ **SANDILANDS**
The Promenade looking South c1955 S480025

A tremendous visual change here is that there are now no breakwater defences along the beach. The bathing huts are still there, and so is the glorious sand. Sandilands can be found just to the south of Sutton on Sea.

▼ **SANDILANDS,** *Sea Lane c1955* S480040

The biggest change is that the shop is now twice as big: it includes the post office, and takes up the whole of the downstairs of the semi-detached house. The house next door with the white bay windows has been covered with what looks like white plastic cladding. During the 1953 storm the flood water was up to window sill level.

▶ **SAXILBY**

High Street c1955 S481021

The whole of the shop extension has been removed, the chimney has gone from the house behind the shop, and it has all been redeveloped. On the other side of the street, the bay-windowed house was a hardware shop, but is a house now; next door the white hut was a blacksmith's, but has since been demolished.

◄ SAXILBY
Foss Dyke c1965
S481024

This is the Roman canal from the Brayford Pool in Lincoln to the river Trent at Torksey, and it is the oldest canal in England. The Lincoln Co-op (centre left) is no longer located here, but in a more modern store at the other end of the village. There are very few shops along the canal side now. However, there are a couple of pubs still in business, the Ship with the sailing ship pub sign and the Sun with a mounting block outside (centre). Boats still tie up alongside, and the pubs do a good trade during the summer months. During the mid 1980s a foot bridge was built beside the other bridge - no doubt a useful and convenient addition.

SKEGNESS
The Clock Tower c1955 S134013

The clock tower was built to celebrate Queen Victoria's Diamond Jubilee in 1898. It now has a much larger traffic island around it, and during the holiday season it is a very busy place indeed. Butlin House (left) has been replaced by a functional modern building. Most of the rest of those buildings are in the main still there, but they do not look as impressive as they did in 1955. The Embassy Ballroom (right) has been greatly altered, and now houses Harveys and the Litton Tree. For safety reasons there is now a wall around the path to keep the people away from the traffic. There is a road crossing nearby.

SKEGNESS
North Shore c1955
S134032

The North Shore of Skegness was slow to develop, but it now has lots of attractions for visitors, including an AstroGlide slide for children. What it does not have now is a helter-skelter and the North Shore Café - all that has gone, and there is now a huge car park here. The distant sand hills and Sea View Walk are still there, and look exactly the same.

SKEGNESS
North Parade c1955
S134043

This a row of typical seaside hotels and boarding houses, and it still looks the same. The only big difference is that the cast iron and glass canopy along the mock-Tudor hotel has all been taken away, and there is now only one shop - and it is not Gallone the Italian ice cream seller, as it is here. The three young ladies, all nicely in step, are still wearing their coats, so it cannot be all that warm. The poster on the right advertises Arcadian Follies at the Pier Pavilion; the pier mainly disappeared in 1978.

▶ **SKEGNESS**
Lumley Road c1955
S134062

Just look at those poor trees! This is the main shopping street, and it leads up to the Victorian clock tower at one end from the railway station at the other. All the shops are still in existence, but the proprietors have changed. The Fun Fair board (right) has gone, and the place is now Coinsville. The Central Café (left) has been replaced by Bon Marche and Multi Choice. Much to a lot of visitors' annoyance, the public toilets that were underground and nearer the clock tower have been demolished. The new ones are further away from the main street.

◀ **SKEGNESS**
The Model Yacht Pond c1955
S134064

At the time of this photograph, the fun fair belonged to Billy Butlin, and the Figure 8 was an exciting ride fifty years ago. Whether you tried the cockles, crabs, mussels, prawns, shrimps or whelks at the Oyster Bar (centre left) before or after you had the ride was entirely up to you. The Figure 8 has been replaced by a ride named Storm. The model yacht pond has shrunk, but is still there. It is all now owned by Bottoms Amusements. Again, what with the coats and caps the weather could not have been too warm.

▲ **SKILLINGTON,** *The Church c1965* S482002

This church has a connection with the Alps! It contains two special glass windows in memory of the Rev Charles Hudson, who lost his life in 1865 during the descent of the Matterhorn. The church of St James, with its broach spire and Anglo-Saxon long and short stone work in the nave, was newly seated and restored in 1854-55.

◄ **SKILLINGTON**
The Village c1965 S482006

This is the Colsterworth Road, and the lane to the left is Lord's Lane - but which Lord it does not state. This is another stone village to the south of Grantham, and houses being built there now must still be stone-faced. The rounded corner house now has lots of roses growing up the wall. The power cables are still there. Skillington is a quiet village nicely off the beaten track.

▼ **SLEAFORD,** *Grantham Road c1965* S483048

This is an attractive approach road into the town centre of Sleaford. The grass verge has gone to make way for a cycle path. The rounded top of St Botolph's Parish Hall, built in 1932, is just visible (right) - strangely enough, it says it is in Quarrington!

► **SLEAFORD**
Southgate c1965 S483049

This is the main shopping street of Sleaford, and the Handley Memorial was the ideal place for a set of destination signs. Things have changed, as there is a one-way system now in operation, and everything goes straight on and to the right of the memorial. Virtually all the shops have changed ownership, but the Nags Head (left) is still providing a pint or two. The Lincoln Co-op (extreme left) has gone, to be replaced by the Job Centre and a Cycle Centre. The small J Corby shop opposite is now Las Vegas Amusements.

◀ SPALDING
In the Bulb Fields
c1955 S388192

It was not only Wordsworth who could see daffodils; we in Lincolnshire can see millions of them at the appropriate time of the year. Around Spalding and Holbeach there are field after field of these beautiful flowers all telling us that spring is here at last. One surprising fact is that we in Lincolnshire grow more daffodils than are grown in Holland.

SPALDING
Ayscoughfee Gardens
c1960 S388222

These gardens are at the rear of Ayscoughfee Hall, which is now in the process of being restored. The building is partly used as the Spalding Tourist Office. The church is the parish church of St Mary and St Nicholas. The pool is now of clear water, and incorporates three fountains. The roofed building has been replaced by the Ayscoughfee Café, and the gardens include an impressive war memorial to Spalding's dead of both wars.

▶ **SPALDING**
Hall Place c1960
S388224

The modern architecture sits very uncomfortably with the earlier buildings – an example is the Fine Fare building, which now houses Super Drug. However, in early 2004 the whole area looked like a builders' yard. The traffic islands and the roads were being replaced by a brick surface. It all had to be finished before the Tulip Parade in early May. The shops are still there, but all have changed owners. Penningtons and the Scotch Wool Shop (right) are now Boots, Martins Bank beyond is now Barclays, and the Co-op (beside Fine Fare) is now Stead & Simpson's. Shoefayre (left) is now Molson & Coakley (optometrists), and finally Sketchley (next door) is now Card Fair.

◀ **SPILSBY**
Market Street c1955
S391001

The name of the pub on the left is still the same - Nelson Butt – but it is now a Free House and no longer belongs to Bateman's. L G Moden next door, a baker of superb bread and mouth-watering Swiss rolls, is no longer there and has been replaced by a Little Italy Restaurant. Shaw's Tea Room is on the right - they advertise jazz nights.

▲ **SPILSBY,** *The Church c1955* S391008

This was the main route through the town until the by-pass came into being. The tower of St James' Church is still the original Spilsby greenstone, but the rest of the church has been faced with the stronger limestone, hence the different colour. Inside are memorials to Sir John Franklin, the great explorer; the Willoughby Chapel contains many tombs, including one in alabaster of John 3rd Baron Willoughby, a distinguished knight who fought under Edward III and the Black Prince.

◄ **SPILSBY**
High Street c1955 S391010

The White Hart (left) contained what was probably the oldest letter box. It was discovered in 1988, and had been in use from 1842. E J Tong the ironmongers next door are still in business and still in the same building, and so is Barclay's Bank. The Midland Bank is now the HSBC; next door, in what was a space in 1955, is now the NFU Mutual organisation.

▼ **SPILSBY,** *Market Place c1955* S391017

Godsmark's (second from left) have been in business and in the same shop for over 80 years, but most of the other businesses have changed. W M Kirk (left) is now Ambridge's Fish and Chip Restaurant. Sketchley, the cleaners have gone, as they have in several little towns. The shop that was S F Chesman (right) is now empty, but Sir John Franklin's statue still stands proudly in the middle of the Market Place and overlooks the Monday market.

▶ **SPILSBY**
The Terrace c1955 S391040

Hilton's shop is still a boot and shoe shop, but Mr O'Connor is the owner. Next door there is now a bookmaker, and the Trustee Savings Bank building now houses Messrs Dexter & Sharp, who are accountants. Even the Cherry Blossom advertisement (left) has disappeared, which is a pity, as it looks so cheerful. The barber's pole (centre right) has also gone.

◄ **STAMFORD**
*St Peter's Callis
c1955* S177022

The word callis means almshouse or hospice, and possibly derives from the name Calais. St Peter's Church was 'pulled down' in 1560, and this building was built in 1863. Both Sheep Market and All Saints Street lead down to what was the Great North Road, but Stamford has since been bypassed. The town bus station is on the right, on the site of Stamford Castle. The church with the tower is St John's. Stamford is classed as the best stone-built town in England.

STAMFORD
St Mary's Hill from the George Hotel c1955
S177035

In the era of the stage coach, the George Hotel was classed as the best hotel on the Great North Road, and it is still one of the best in the area. The car park is still on the left, and the gallows sign is still over the road. Between the sign and St Mary's Church is the Town Bridge over the river Welland. Even the steps and the handrail are still in situ, but the shop window on the right has gone.

STAMFORD

St Paul's Street c1955 S177064

This has to be one of the most attractive roof lines in England, and with snow would make a perfect Christmas card. The chapel of Stamford School is hiding among the trees: it was originally the church of St Paul. All the businesses have changed, but the buildings have not. Chapman's the shoe repairer's (left) is now Rutland Fishing; next is now a book shop, and then comes the Royal Restaurant. Sidney Hudson the baker has been replaced by Simpole Clark, fine foods. The window cleaner is outside a house which has a plaque inscribed 'Joseph and Jane Caldecott 1714', but the house is much older than that. The other sign is for the RAF Association, who hold their meetings there. The garage on the right was no longer in business when this research was being done.

STAMFORD, *High Street c1960* S177118

Now pedestrianised, this is the main shopping street of Stamford. Woolworth's have expanded to take over the Pine Apple Pub (right), a most unusual name for a pub. Stead & Simpson's are next door to what was Maypole (left) but now is the Edinburgh Wool shop, and Walkers Books are now beyond in what was Parrish & Son, clothiers. The Halifax Bank reconstructed the historic building next door to Parrish in 1982 and did a good job.

SURFLEET, *The Church c1955* S504010

Pisa is famous for its leaning tower, but Surfleet's church of St Lawrence is a notable south Lincolnshire rival, as it leans considerably towards the A152 main road despite two very robust buttresses. The River Glen is just over the wall flowing towards the Wash, and the church pathways are prettily lined by many daffodils in springtime.

SUTTON ON SEA
The Beach c1965 S235127

Yet another beautiful Lincolnshire sandy beach, and yet again the wooden breakwater defences have been taken away. The sea appears to be calm and the weather is warm. With deck chairs, buckets, spades and ball, everything is set for an ideal day at the seaside.

105

► **SUTTON ON SEA**
*The Garden Café
c1955* S235045

The name is still there, but the building is not. The Garden Café is now underneath the chalets; on this site is now a water fountain feature. However, the concrete steps are still visible.

◄ **TATTERSHALL**
The Buttercross c1955
T15008

The Buttercross is to be found in the centre of the village market place. The railings have gone, as have the brick wall and the trees behind it. The shop under the white blind is now named Something Fishy. Tattershall has lost its railway, but it still has its castle, and Tom Thumb's house is still on top of a house on the left of the market place.

▲ **TATTERSHALL,** *The Bedehouses c1955* T15011

These old houses are to be found in the shadow of Tattershall Castle and next to the collegiate church of the Holy Trinity. Founded in 1440, these houses were altered in 1967 making two units into one, thereby enabling more modern kitchens to be installed. The churchyard is much more tidy now.

◄ **TEALBY**
The Village c1960
T216018

Tealby has the reputation of being Lincolnshire's most beautiful village, and as beauty is in the eye of the beholder it may well be, as it truly is picturesque. It is only a few miles from Market Rasen on the way to Grimsby, and is well worth a visit.

▲ **TRUSTHORPE**
The Beach c1955 T217015

Oh, how we love to make sand castles just so that our children can knock then down or jump on them. Here we have only two more to go! The cannon would not have been much use in 1940. Mablethorpe is to the right and north.

108

TRUSTHORPE
Trusville c1955
T217047

We have entered the age of the motor car! The village of Trusthorpe is located between Mablethorpe and Sutton on Sea, and Trusville was developed after the war. This area is now mainly caravans and chalets. The tower in the background is of the church of St Peter in Trusthorpe village.

WADDINGTON, *The Wheatsheaf Inn c1960* W2013

This stone-built pub on the main road between Grantham and Lincoln was probably built in the 18th century as a farmhouse. It was a very popular 'watering hole' for aircrews from the nearby aerodrome, and has numerous old and new photographs to remember those days. Members of the RAF and the RAAF are remembered by a memorial clock located in the shopping precinct, and dedicated to those who did not return from operations over enemy territory.

► **WAINFLEET ALL SAINTS**
Market Place c1955
W550001

The buildings have not changed in fifty years - except that no one can remember the clock tower (built in 1899) not having a top to it! Wilkinson's (right) is now Storrs, and Robbialac paint is no longer available. The white building beyond now houses pizzas and kebabs, accountants, and antiques. The corner stationer's is still just that. The market day is Friday. The whole square is the property of the Duchy of Lancaster, states a notice in the shelter in the middle of the square.

◄ **WAINFLEET ALL SAINTS**
High Street c1955
W550017

The Nottingham Co-operative Society (centre) is no longer on the left of the High Street - the building is now a pet shop, and the Co-op has moved to a more modern building across the street. Barton the grocer's (left) is now Snips and Clips, and Scupholm, the potato merchant next door, is now The Filling Station, a good sandwich shop. The Angel Inn is in the distance.

▲ **WAINFLEET ALL SAINTS,** *The River c1955* W550004

This is the Steeping river flowing towards the Wash and the North Sea. Earlier in its life it had more publicity, as it is also known as Tennyson's brook. There is no change in this beautiful and tranquil scene as the river gently flows by the lovely thatched house onwards to Gibraltar Point.

◄ **WELLINGORE**
Wellingore Hall c1960
W513012

The central part of this prominent building was built in c1750, and the two outer bays were added in the early 19th century. The chapel was added in 1878 and rebuilt after a fire in 1885. It is now all offices, and the Roman Catholic chapel has been deconsecrated. The biggest tenant is now the St John's Ambulance. There are fine views from the building over the Trent and Witham valley.

111

WELLINGORE
The Church c1960
W513015

All Saints' Church stands proudly at the top of a sharp double bend and hill on the A607 road going towards Lincoln from Grantham. It is another of the village churches built of the limestone from the ridge that acts as a spine all the way through Lincolnshire from Stamford up to the river Humber.

WOODHALL SPA, *The Broadway c1960* W362033

This is the main shopping street through Woodhall Spa. There was a railway crossing across the street in the distance. W H Smith (right) has gone, and since 1994 the shop has been owned by an antiques dealer. The van (left) is coming out of Stanhope Avenue. Woodhall Spa is really a holiday town in the middle of Lincolnshire for people dedicated to golf.

WOODHALL SPA
The Golf Hotel c1965
W362035

The recent news is that spa water has been found about six hundred feet down, and the Golf Hotel is about to resurrect the spa baths sometime during 2005. The building was formerly the Clevedon House Preparatory School and a boarding school for boys. Almost next door to this attractive hotel is the English National Golf Centre. The Woodhall Spa golf course has been voted the best inland course in England.

WOODHALL SPA, *Jubilee Park Swimming Pool c1965* W362041

HRH Princess Marie Louise opened the park in April 1935 to commemorate the Silver Jubilee of King George V - the plaque stating this information is on the side of the cafeteria. The pool is a heated outdoor pool; the fountain has gone. There is a large caravan site here, and a children's play area. The park caters for cricket, tennis, and bowls, and it has a putting green. This is a marvellous asset for the community.

WOOLSTHORPE BY BELVOIR
The Village c1955 W363007

Nothing much has altered here except that the Narrow Road sign has been changed and there are some new power lines across the road. Even the wooden gate (centre) is newer, but of the same functional design. Many of the village houses are built of the local ironstone; this gives them a rusty red colour, the same as the houses in Denton. The long roof of the church is visible as we look towards the village centre.

WOOLSTHORPE BY BELVOIR, *The Village c1955* W363019

This is the village centre. The main change is that the large tree has been replaced by a pub sign, which now forms the centrepiece of a large round traffic island incorporating an attractive floral feature. The houses to the right have also been replaced by those of a more modern design. There are two Woolsthorpes in Lincolnshire, and they are not far apart. This one nestles under the shadow of Belvoir Castle; the other is the one with the Sir Isaac Newton connections, and is situated near Colsterworth.

INDEX

Frith Book Co Titles

www.francisfrith.co.uk

The Frith Book Company publishes over 100 new titles each year. A selection of those currently available is listed below. For latest catalogue please contact Frith Book Co.

Town Books 96 pages, approximately 100 photos. **County and Themed Books** 128 pages, approximately 150 photos (unless specified). All titles hardback with laminated case and jacket except those indicated pb (paperback)

Amersham, Chesham & Rickmansworth (pb)	1-85937-340-2	£9.99	Devon (pb)	1-85937-297-x	£9.9
Andover (pb)	1-85937-292-9	£9.99	Devon Churches (pb)	1-85937-250-3	£9.9
Aylesbury (pb)	1-85937-227-9	£9.99	Dorchester (pb)	1-85937-307-0	£9.9
Barnstaple (pb)	1-85937-300-3	£9.99	Dorset (pb)	1-85937-269-4	£9.9
Basildon Living Memories (pb)	1-85937-515-4	£9.99	Dorset Coast (pb)	1-85937-299-6	£9.9
Bath (pb)	1-85937-419-0	£9.99	Dorset Living Memories (pb)	1-85937-584-7	£9.9
Bedford (pb)	1-85937-205-8	£9.99	Down the Severn (pb)	1-85937-560-x	£9.9
Bedfordshire Living Memories	1-85937-513-8	£14.99	Down The Thames (pb)	1-85937-278-3	£9.9
Belfast (pb)	1-85937-303-8	£9.99	Down the Trent	1-85937-311-9	£14.9
Berkshire (pb)	1-85937-191-4	£9.99	East Anglia (pb)	1-85937-265-1	£9.9
Berkshire Churches	1-85937-170-1	£17.99	East Grinstead (pb)	1-85937-138-8	£9.9
Berkshire Living Memories	1-85937-332-1	£14.99	East London	1-85937-080-2	£14.9
Black Country	1-85937-497-2	£12.99	East Sussex (pb)	1-85937-606-1	£9.9
Blackpool (pb)	1-85937-393-3	£9.99	Eastbourne (pb)	1-85937-399-2	£9.9
Bognor Regis (pb)	1-85937-431-x	£9.99	Edinburgh (pb)	1-85937-193-0	£8.9
Bournemouth (pb)	1-85937-545-6	£9.99	England In The 1880s	1-85937-331-3	£17.9
Bradford (pb)	1-85937-204-x	£9.99	Essex - Second Selection	1-85937-456-5	£14.9
Bridgend (pb)	1-85937-386-0	£7.99	Essex (pb)	1-85937-270-8	£9.9
Bridgwater (pb)	1-85937-305-4	£9.99	Essex Coast	1-85937-342-9	£14.9
Bridport (pb)	1-85937-327-5	£9.99	Essex Living Memories	1-85937-490-5	£14.9
Brighton (pb)	1-85937-192-2	£8.99	Exeter	1-85937-539-1	£9.9
Bristol (pb)	1-85937-264-3	£9.99	Exmoor (pb)	1-85937-608-8	£9.9
British Life A Century Ago (pb)	1-85937-213-9	£9.99	Falmouth (pb)	1-85937-594-4	£9.9
Buckinghamshire (pb)	1-85937-200-7	£9.99	Folkestone (pb)	1-85937-124-8	£9.9
Camberley (pb)	1-85937-222-8	£9.99	Frome (pb)	1-85937-317-8	£9.9
Cambridge (pb)	1-85937-422-0	£9.99	Glamorgan	1-85937-488-3	£14.9
Cambridgeshire (pb)	1-85937-420-4	£9.99	Glasgow (pb)	1-85937-190-6	£9.9
Cambridgeshire Villages	1-85937-523-5	£14.99	Glastonbury (pb)	1-85937-338-0	£7.9
Canals And Waterways (pb)	1-85937-291-0	£9.99	Gloucester (pb)	1-85937-232-5	£9.9
Canterbury Cathedral (pb)	1-85937-179-5	£9.99	Gloucestershire (pb)	1-85937-561-8	£9.9
Cardiff (pb)	1-85937-093-4	£9.99	Great Yarmouth (pb)	1-85937-426-3	£9.9
Carmarthenshire (pb)	1-85937-604-5	£9.99	Greater Manchester (pb)	1-85937-266-x	£9.9
Chelmsford (pb)	1-85937-310-0	£9.99	Guildford (pb)	1-85937-410-7	£9.9
Cheltenham (pb)	1-85937-095-0	£9.99	Hampshire (pb)	1-85937-279-1	£9.9
Cheshire (pb)	1-85937-271-6	£9.99	Harrogate (pb)	1-85937-423-9	£9.9
Chester (pb)	1-85937-382 8	£9.99	Hastings and Bexhill (pb)	1-85937-131-0	£9.9
Chesterfield (pb)	1-85937-378-x	£9.99	Heart of Lancashire (pb)	1-85937-197-3	£9.9
Chichester (pb)	1-85937-228-7	£9.99	Helston (pb)	1-85937-214-7	£9.9
Churches of East Cornwall (pb)	1-85937-249-x	£9.99	Hereford (pb)	1-85937-175-2	£9.9
Churches of Hampshire (pb)	1-85937-207-4	£9.99	Herefordshire (pb)	1-85937-567-7	£9.9
Cinque Ports & Two Ancient Towns	1-85937-492-1	£14.99	Herefordshire Living Memories	1-85937-514-6	£14.9
Colchester (pb)	1-85937-188-4	£8.99	Hertfordshire (pb)	1-85937-247-3	£9.9
Cornwall (pb)	1-85937-229-5	£9.99	Horsham (pb)	1-85937-432-8	£9.9
Cornwall Living Memories	1-85937-248-1	£14.99	Humberside (pb)	1-85937-605-3	£9.9
Cotswolds (pb)	1-85937-230-9	£9.99	Hythe, Romney Marsh, Ashford (pb)	1-85937-256-2	£9.9
Cotswolds Living Memories	1-85937-255-4	£14.99	Ipswich (pb)	1-85937-424-7	£9.9
County Durham (pb)	1-85937-398-4	£9.99	Isle of Man (pb)	1-85937-268-6	£9.9
Croydon Living Memories (pb)	1-85937-162-0	£9.99	Isle of Wight (pb)	1-85937-429-8	£9.9
Cumbria (pb)	1-85937-621-5	£9.99	Isle of Wight Living Memories	1-85937-304-6	£14.9
Derby (pb)	1-85937-367-4	£9.99	Kent (pb)	1-85937-189-2	£9.9
Derbyshire (pb)	1-85937-196-5	£9.99	Kent Living Memories(pb)	1-85937-401-8	£9.9
Derbyshire Living Memories	1-85937-330-5	£14.99	Kings Lynn (pb)	1-85937-334-8	£9.9

Available from your local bookshop or from the publisher

Frith Book Co Titles (continued)

Title	ISBN	Price	Title	ISBN	Price
ke District (pb)	1-85937-275-9	£9.99	Sherborne (pb)	1-85937-301-1	£9.99
ncashire Living Memories	1-85937-335-6	£14.99	Shrewsbury (pb)	1-85937-325-9	£9.99
ncaster, Morecambe, Heysham (pb)	1-85937-233-3	£9.99	Shropshire (pb)	1-85937-326-7	£9.99
eds (pb)	1-85937-202-3	£9.99	Shropshire Living Memories	1-85937-643-6	£14.99
icester (pb)	1-85937-381-x	£9.99	Somerset	1-85937-153-1	£14.99
icestershire & Rutland Living Memories	1-85937-500-6	£12.99	South Devon Coast	1-85937-107-8	£14.99
icestershire (pb)	1-85937-185-x	£9.99	South Devon Living Memories (pb)	1-85937-609-6	£9.99
ghthouses	1-85937-257-0	£9.99	South East London (pb)	1-85937-263-5	£9.99
ncoln (pb)	1-85937-380-1	£9.99	South Somerset	1-85937-318-6	£14.99
ncolnshire (pb)	1-85937-433-6	£9.99	South Wales	1-85937-519-7	£14.99
verpool and Merseyside (pb)	1-85937-234-1	£9.99	Southampton (pb)	1-85937-427-1	£9.99
ndon (pb)	1-85937-183-3	£9.99	Southend (pb)	1-85937-313-5	£9.99
ndon Living Memories	1-85937-454-9	£14.99	Southport (pb)	1-85937-425-5	£9.99
dlow (pb)	1-85937-176-0	£9.99	St Albans (pb)	1-85937-341-0	£9.99
ton (pb)	1-85937-235-x	£9.99	St Ives (pb)	1-85937-415-8	£9.99
aidenhead (pb)	1-85937-339-9	£9.99	Stafford Living Memories (pb)	1-85937-503-0	£9.99
aidstone (pb)	1-85937-391-7	£9.99	Staffordshire (pb)	1-85937-308-9	£9.99
anchester (pb)	1-85937-198-1	£9.99	Stourbridge (pb)	1-85937-530-8	£9.99
arlborough (pb)	1-85937-336-4	£9.99	Stratford upon Avon (pb)	1-85937-388-7	£9.99
iddlesex	1-85937-158-2	£14.99	Suffolk (pb)	1-85937-221-x	£9.99
onmouthshire	1-85937-532-4	£14.99	Suffolk Coast (pb)	1-85937-610-x	£9.99
ew Forest (pb)	1-85937-390-9	£9.99	Surrey (pb)	1-85937-240-6	£9.99
ewark (pb)	1-85937-366-6	£9.99	Surrey Living Memories	1-85937-328-3	£14.99
ewport, Wales (pb)	1-85937-258-9	£9.99	Sussex (pb)	1-85937-184-1	£9.99
ewquay (pb)	1-85937-421-2	£9.99	Sutton (pb)	1-85937-337-2	£9.99
orfolk (pb)	1-85937-195-7	£9.99	Swansea (pb)	1-85937-167-1	£9.99
orfolk Broads	1-85937-486-7	£14.99	Taunton (pb)	1-85937-314-3	£9.99
orfolk Living Memories (pb)	1-85937-402-6	£9.99	Tees Valley & Cleveland (pb)	1-85937-623-1	£9.99
orth Buckinghamshire	1-85937-626-6	£14.99	Teignmouth (pb)	1-85937-370-4	£7.99
orth Devon Living Memories	1-85937-261-9	£14.99	Thanet (pb)	1-85937-116-7	£9.99
orth Hertfordshire	1-85937-547-2	£14.99	Tiverton (pb)	1-85937-178-7	£9.99
orth London (pb)	1-85937-403-4	£9.99	Torbay (pb)	1-85937-597-9	£9.99
orth Somerset	1-85937-302-x	£14.99	Truro (pb)	1-85937-598-7	£9.99
orth Wales (pb)	1-85937-298-8	£9.99	Victorian & Edwardian Dorset	1-85937-254-6	£14.99
orth Yorkshire (pb)	1-85937-236-8	£9.99	Victorian & Edwardian Kent (pb)	1-85937-624-X	£9.99
orthamptonshire Living Memories	1-85937-529-4	£14.99	Victorian & Edwardian Maritime Album (pb)	1-85937-622-3	£9.99
orthamptonshire	1-85937-150-7	£14.99	Victorian and Edwardian Sussex (pb)	1-85937-625-8	£9.99
orthumberland Tyne & Wear (pb)	1-85937-281-3	£9.99	Villages of Devon (pb)	1-85937-293-7	£9.99
orthumberland	1-85937-522-7	£14.99	Villages of Kent (pb)	1-85937-294-5	£9.99
orwich (pb)	1-85937-194-9	£8.99	Villages of Sussex (pb)	1-85937-295-3	£9.99
ottingham (pb)	1-85937-324-0	£9.99	Warrington (pb)	1-85937-507-3	£9.99
ottinghamshire (pb)	1-85937-187-6	£9.99	Warwick (pb)	1-85937-518-9	£9.99
xford (pb)	1-85937-411-5	£9.99	Warwickshire (pb)	1-85937-203-1	£9.99
xfordshire (pb)	1-85937-430-1	£9.99	Welsh Castles (pb)	1-85937-322-4	£9.99
xfordshire Living Memories	1-85937-525-1	£14.99	West Midlands (pb)	1-85937-289-9	£9.99
aignton (pb)	1-85937-374-7	£7.99	West Sussex (pb)	1-85937-607-x	£9.99
eak District (pb)	1-85937-280-5	£9.99	West Yorkshire (pb)	1-85937-201-5	£9.99
embrokeshire	1-85937-262-7	£14.99	Weston Super Mare (pb)	1-85937-306-2	£9.99
enzance (pb)	1-85937-595-2	£9.99	Weymouth (pb)	1-85937-209-0	£9.99
eterborough (pb)	1-85937-219-8	£9.99	Wiltshire (pb)	1-85937-277-5	£9.99
cturesque Harbours	1-85937-208-2	£14.99	Wiltshire Churches (pb)	1-85937-171-x	£9.99
ers	1 85937-237-6	£17.99	Wiltshire Living Memories (pb)	1-85937-396-8	£9.99
ymouth (pb)	1-85937-389-5	£9.99	Winchester (pb)	1-85937-428-x	£9.99
ole & Sandbanks (pb)	1-85937-251-1	£9.99	Windsor (pb)	1-85937-333-x	£9.99
eston (pb)	1-85937-212-0	£9.99	Wokingham & Bracknell (pb)	1-85937-329-1	£9.99
eading (pb)	1-85937-238-4	£9.99	Woodbridge (pb)	1-85937-498-0	£9.99
edhill to Reigate (pb)	1-85937-596-0	£9.99	Worcester (pb)	1-85937-165-5	£9.99
ngwood (pb)	1-85937-384-4	£7.99	Worcestershire Living Memories	1-85937-489-1	£14.99
omford (pb)	1-85937-319-4	£9.99	Worcestershire	1-85937-152-3	£14.99
oyal Tunbridge Wells (pb)	1-85937-504-9	£9.99	York (pb)	1-85937-199-x	£9.99
alisbury (pb)	1-85937-239-2	£9.99	Yorkshire (pb)	1-85937-186-8	£9.99
carborough (pb)	1-85937-379-8	£9.99	Yorkshire Coastal Memories	1-85937-506-5	£14.99
evenoaks and Tonbridge (pb)	1-85937-392-5	£9.99	Yorkshire Dales	1-85937-502-2	£14.99
heffield & South Yorks (pb)	1-85937-267-8	£9.99	Yorkshire Living Memories (pb)	1-85937-397-6	£9.99

See Frith books on the internet at www.francisfrith.co.uk

FRITH PRODUCTS & SERVICES

Francis Frith would doubtless be pleased to know that the pioneering publishing venture he started in 1860 still continues today. Over a hundred and forty years later, The Francis Frith Collection continues in the same innovative tradition and is now one of the foremost publishers of vintage photographs in the world. Some of the current activities include:

Interior Decoration

Today Frith's photographs can be seen framed and as giant wall murals in thousands of pubs, restaurants, hotels, banks, retail stores and other public buildings throughout the country. In every case they enhance the unique local atmosphere of the places they depict and provide reminders of gentler days in an increasingly busy and frenetic world.

Product Promotions

Frith products are used by many major companies to promote the sales of their own products or to reinforce their own history and heritage. Frith promotions have been used by Hovis bread, Courage beers, Scots Porage Oats, Colman's mustard, Cadbury's foods, Mellow Birds coffee, Dunhill pipe tobacco, Guinness, and Bulmer's Cider.

Genealogy and Family History

As the interest in family history and roots grows world-wide, more and more people are turning to Frith's photographs of Great Britain for images of the towns, villages and streets where their ancestors lived; and, of course, photographs of the churches and chapels where their ancestors were christened, married and buried are an essential part of every genealogy tree and family album.

Frith Products

All Frith photographs are available Framed or just as Mounted Prints and Posters (size 23 x 16 inches). These may be ordered from the address below. From time to time other products - Address Books, Calendars, Table Mats, etc - are available.

The Internet

Already fifty thousand Frith photographs can be viewed and purchased on the internet through the Frith websites and a myriad of partner sites.

For more detailed information on Frith companies and products, look at these sites:

www.francisfrith.co.uk
www.francisfrith.com
(for North American visitors)

See the complete list of Frith Books at:

www.francisfrith.co.uk

This web site is regularly updated with the latest list of publications from the Frith Book Company. If you wish to buy books relating to another part of the country that your local bookshop does not stock, you may purchase on-line.

For further information, trade, or author enquiries please contact us at the address below:
The Francis Frith Collection, Frith's Barn, Teffont, Salisbury, Wiltshire, England SP3 5QP.
Tel: +44 (0)1722 716 376 Fax: +44 (0)1722 716 881 Email: sales@francisfrith.co.uk

See Frith books on the internet at www.francisfrith.co.uk

FREE MOUNTED PRINT

Mounted Print
Overall size 14 x 11 inches

Fill in and cut out this voucher and return
it with your remittance for £2.25 (to cover postage and handling). Offer valid for delivery to UK addresses only.

Choose any photograph included in this book.
Your SEPIA print will be A4 in size. It will be mounted in a cream mount with a burgundy rule line (overall size 14 x 11 inches).

Order additional Mounted Prints at HALF PRICE (only £7.49 each*)
If you would like to order more Frith prints from this book, possibly as gifts for friends and family, you can buy them at half price (with no additional postage and handling costs).

Have your Mounted Prints framed
For an extra £14.95 per print* you can have your mounted print(s) framed in an elegant polished wood and gilt moulding, overall size 16 x 13 inches (no additional postage and handling required).

---

* IMPORTANT!

These special prices are only available if you order at the same time as you order your free mounted print. You must use the ORIGINAL VOUCHER on this page (no copies permitted). We can only despatch to one address.

Send completed Voucher form to:
The Francis Frith Collection, Frith's Barn, Teffont, Salisbury, Wiltshire SP3 5QP

CHOOSE ANY IMAGE FROM THIS BOOK

Voucher **for FREE** *and Reduced Price Frith Prints*

Please do not photocopy this voucher. Only the original is valid, so please fill it in, cut it out and return it to us with your order.

Picture ref no	Page no	Qty	Mounted @ £7.49	Framed + £14.95	Total Cost
		1	Free of charge*	£	£
			£7.49	£	£
			£7.49	£	£
			£7.49	£	£
			£7.49	£	£
			£7.49	£	£

Please allow 28 days for delivery

* Post & handling (UK)	£2.25
Total Order Cost	£

Title of this book . . . .

I enclose a cheque/postal order for £ . . . .

made payable to 'The Francis Frith Collection'

OR please debit my Mastercard / Visa / Switch / Amex card

(credit cards please on all overseas orders), details below

Card Number

Issue No (Switch only)   Valid from (Amex/Switch)

Expires   Signature

Name Mr/Mrs/Ms . . . .

Address . . . .

. . . .

. . . .

. . . . Postcode . . . .

Daytime Tel No . . . .

Email . . . .

Valid to 31/12/05

Free Print – see overleaf

Would you like to find out more about Francis Frith?

We have recently recruited some entertaining speakers who are happy to visit local groups, clubs and societies to give an illustrated talk documenting Frith's travels and photographs. If you are a member of such a group and are interested in hosting a presentation, we would love to hear from you.

Our speakers bring with them a small selection of our local town and county books, together with sample prints. They are happy to take orders. A small proportion of the order value is donated to the group who have hosted the presentation. The talks are therefore an excellent way of fundraising for small groups and societies.

Can you help us with information about any of the Frith photographs in this book?

We are gradually compiling an historical record for each of the photographs in the Frith archive. It is always fascinating to find out the names of the people shown in the pictures, as well as insights into the shops, buildings and other features depicted.

If you recognize anyone in the photographs in this book, or if you have information not already included in the author's caption, do let us know. We would love to hear from you, and will try to publish it in future books or articles.

Our production team

Frith books are produced by a small dedicated team at offices in the converted Grade II listed 18th-century barn at Teffont near Salisbury, illustrated above. Most have worked with the Frith Collection for many years. All have in common one quality: they have a passion for the Frith Collection. The team is constantly expanding, but currently includes:

Paul Baron, Jason Buck, John Buck, Ruth Butler, Heather Crisp, David Davies, Isobel Hall, Julian Hight, Peter Horne, James Kinnear, Karen Kinnear, Tina Leary, Stuart Login, David Marsh, Sue Molloy, Glenda Morgan, Wayne Morgan, Kate Rotondetto, Dean Scourse, Eliza Sackett, Terence Sackett, Sandra Sampson, Adrian Sanders, Sandra Sanger, Julia Skinner, Claire Tarrier, Lewis Taylor, Shelley Tolcher, Lorraine Tuck and Jeremy Walker.